D0598802

# RUBBER BAND

# BRACELET FUN

Learn to make a triple rainbow bracelet, triple beaded bracelet, a flower ring, a flower bracelet, and a beaded flower bracelet.

*Written by: Julie Rudinski*

*Illustrated by:*
*Julie & Chris Rudinski*

This guide shows you how to make four Bracelet styles and a ring using the Rainbow Loom © 2012 Choon's Design LLC.

# Contents

# Starting Configuration

There should be 3 rows, the right and left row are parallel to each other with a row in the center that is slightly higher. The pegs should all be facing the same direction.

# Tips and Tricks

- PRACTICE PRACTICE PRACTICE. Don't be discouraged if the bracelets don't appear right when you first make them. It takes a lot of practice to learn these advanced designs.
- You can use a thin sharpie to color in the clear arrows on your loom in order to better see them.
- When placing the rubber bands on to the loom always position the loom so that the arrows are facing away from you.
- When hooking the rubber bands make sure the arrows on the loom are facing towards you.
- Push the rubber bands as far down on the loom as possible. This is especially helpful on the flower design as you need the room to add additional rubber bands.
- ALWAYS unhook the rubber bands from the inside of the other rubber bands on the peg.
- When unhooking the rubber bands, hold the loom tool so that the hook is facing away from you. Use the back of the hook to pull the bands back away from the loom allowing you room to grab the correct rubber band.
- When using this guide always hook and unhook in the direction of the arrows. When used, follow the numbered diagrams for the correct band placement.

# Common Steps

## Hooking Bands

When hooking the bands make sure the loom arrows are facing AWAY from you.

Place the rubber band on the first peg.

Stretch the rubber band straight ahead, so that the band wraps around the two peg. Repeat steps 1 & 2 until all pegs necessary for the design have bands. When placing the bands on the pegs be sure to overlap them.

For example place the first rubber band on peg # 1 and then stretch to peg # 2. Place the next band on peg # 2 and stretch it to forward to peg # 3.

## Unhooking Bands

When unhooking the bands make sure the loom arrows are facing TOWARDS you.

You will do the same basic process as hooking the bands to unhook them. However you will always go in the opposite direction.

Use the loom tool to grab the rubber band on the first peg closest to you. Grab the band from the center of the loom peg, Be sure to go on the inside of any bands that may also be on this peg. Unhook the band from the peg it is on and pull it forward, hooking it onto the peg in front of it. The band will now have its start and end on the same peg, but it should have other bands sandwiched between it.

This is the way the bracelets hook together and stay in one piece once removed from the loom. If the bracelet falls apart when removed from the loom, it is most likely that you grabbed the bad from the outside of the peg.

# Make an Infinity Band

## Step 1

Take a rubber band and place it around two fingers

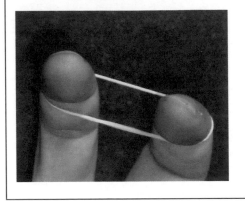

## Step 2

Twist the band making the number 8 or infinity sign.

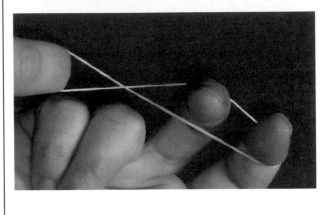

## Step 3

Wrap the band back over your two fingers.

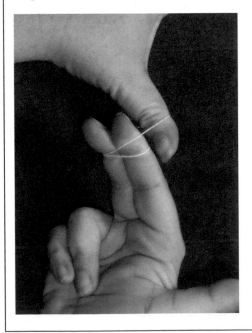

## Step 4

Place the band on the loom.

# Make an Extension Band

## Step 1

With the arrows facing towards you, locate the last peg on the loom in the middle row. Insert the loom tool inside all the rubber bands.

## Step 2

Place a rubber band on the end of the hook.

## Step 3

Pull the rubber band back through the rubber bands on the peg.

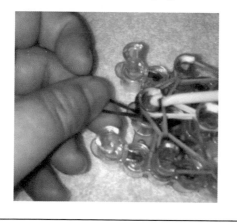

## Step 4

Place both sides of the rubber band on the loom tool. Make sure the band goes around all the other bands on this peg, as this will help your bracelet stay together. Leave the rubber band on the tool until you add the bracelet to the extension. You can now remove the bracelet from the loom.

# TRIPLE RAINBOW BRACELET

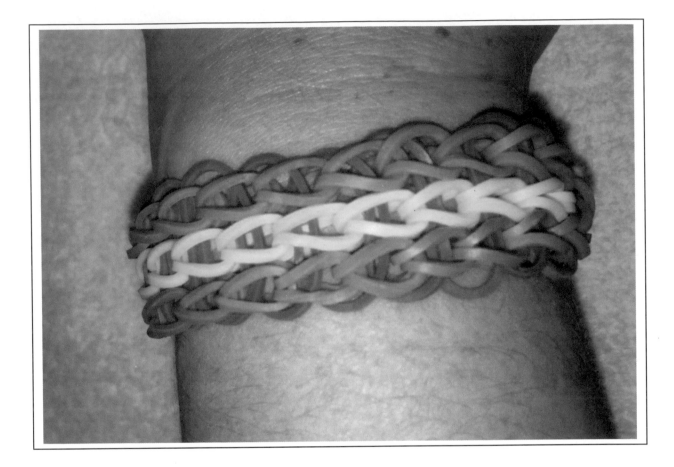

# Step 1

Position the loom so that the arrows are away from you. Place the rubber bands. Start at the middle peg and go diagonal to the left, then continue straight up the loom.

Once you get to the last peg, go diagonal back to the center.

# Step 2

Place the rubber bands. Start at the middle peg and go diagonal to the right, then continue straight up the loom.

Once you get to the last peg, go diagonal back to the center.

# Step 3

Start at the middle peg and place the rubber bands going straight up.

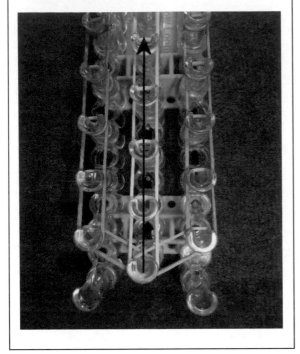

# Step 4

Starting from the 3 peg up on the left hand side, place a rubber bang going straight across to the right side peg.

# Step 5

Pull the rubber band down to the middle peg, making a triangle.

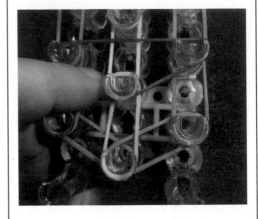

Continue placing the triangle rubber bands up the loom. Place 10 triangle rubber bands at the 3rd – 12 the peg.

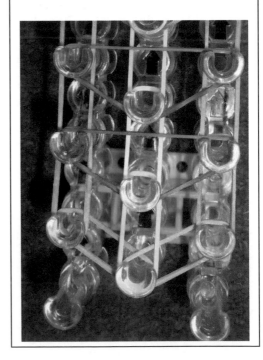

# Step 6

Place an infinity band on the peg at each end of the loom.

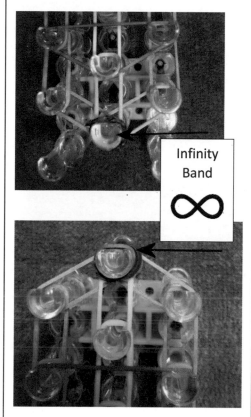

Infinity Band

∞

See Common Steps section for instructions on making the infinity band.

# Step 7

Rotate the loom so that the arrows are now pointing towards you and begin the unhooking process. Starting at the middle peg and continuing straight up.

Make sure you unhook the rubber band from inside the other rubber bands. You may have to hold the infinity band down with your finger so that it does not become unhooked from the peg.

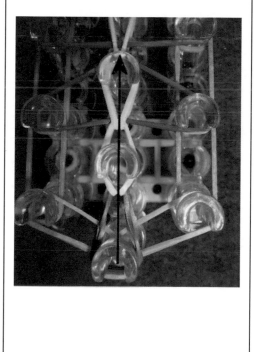

# Step 8

Unhook the left side of the loom. Start at the middle peg and go diagonal to the left, then continue unhooking straight up the loom.

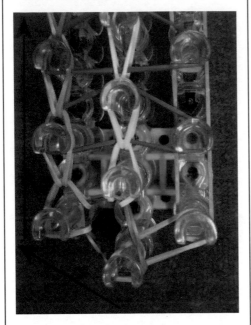

Once you get to the last peg, go diagonal back to the center.

# Step 9

Unhook the right side of the loom. Start at the middle peg and go diagonal to the right, then continue unhooking straight up the loom.

Once you get to the last peg, go diagonal back to the center.

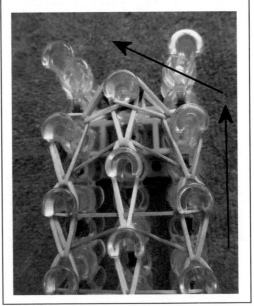

# Step 10

Place an extension band on the end of the bracelet (see common steps for instructions on how to do this.) Leave the loom tool attached to the bracelet.

Remove the bracelet from the loom.

# Step 11

Position the loom with the arrows facing away from you. Place 5 Bands going up in a row. It does not matter which row of the loom you decide to use.

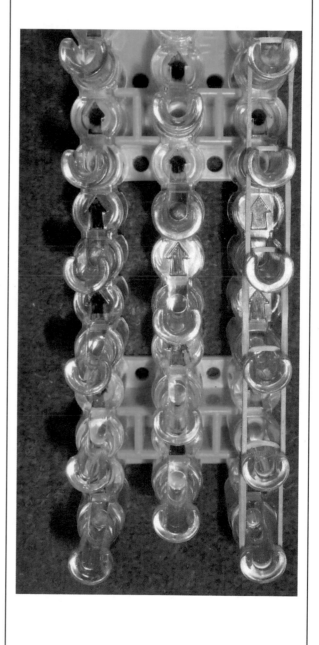

# Step 12

Place the bracelet on the last two pegs of the row using the extension band. Once the bracelet is on the loom, you can remove the loom tool. Then turn the loom so that the arrows are facing towards you.

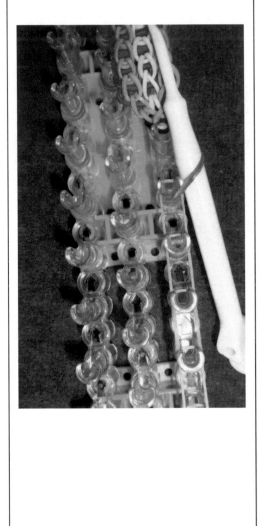

# Step 13

Unhook the bands going in a straight line to the next peg. Place a C-Clip on the end. Remove bracelet from the loom and connect the other end of the bracelet to the C-Clip.

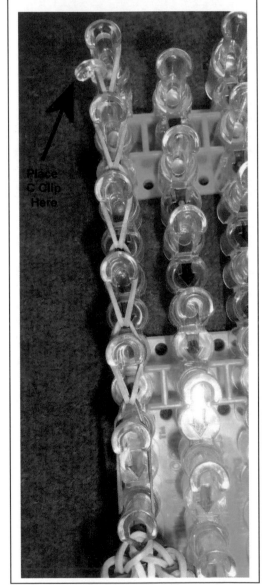

Place C-Clip Here

# BEADED BONANZA BRACELET

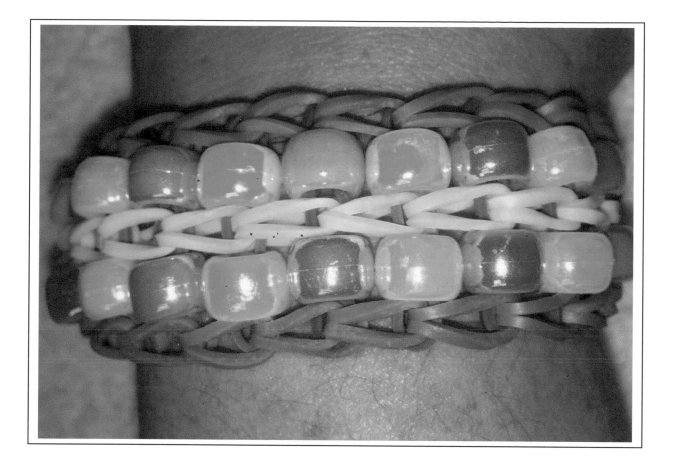

# Step 1

Position the loom so that the arrows are facing away from you. Place the rubber bands. Start at the middle peg and go diagonal to the left, then continue straight up the loom.

Once you get to the last peg, go diagonal back to the center.

# Step 2

Place the rubber bands. Start at the middle peg and go diagonal to the right, then continue straight up the loom.

Once you get to the last peg, go diagonal back to the center.

# Step 3

Start at the middle peg and place the rubber bands going straight up.

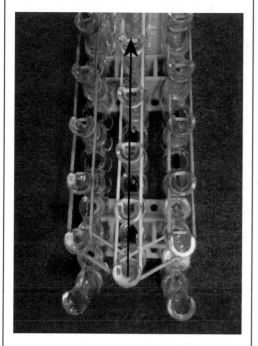

# Step 4

String 2 beads on a rubber band

# Step 5

Starting on the second peg from the bottom, stretch the beaded rubber band straight across the loom. Make sure the beads sit on each side of the middle band.

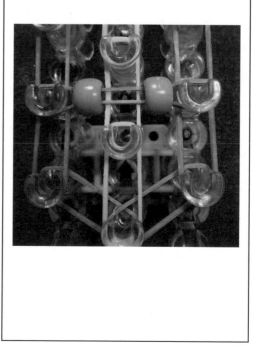

# Step 6

Take the bottom rubber band and stretch it to the middle peg directly below the rubber band forming a triangle.

# Step 7

Continue placing the triangle rubber bands up the loom. Place 10 triangle rubber bands at the 3rd – 12 the peg .

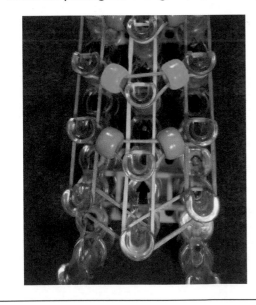
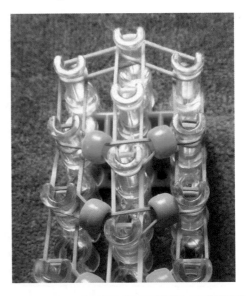

# Step 8

Place infinity bands at the start and end points. (See Common Steps for instructions on making an infinity band).

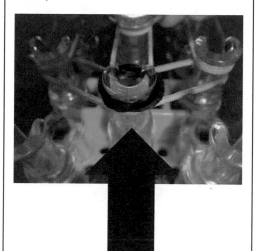

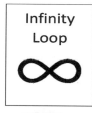

Infinity Loop

# Step 9

Rotate the loom so that the arrows are now pointing towards you and begin the unhooking process. Starting at the middle peg and continuing straight up.

Make sure you unhook the rubber band from inside the other rubber bands.

You may have to hold the infinity band down with your finger so that it does not become unhooked from the peg.

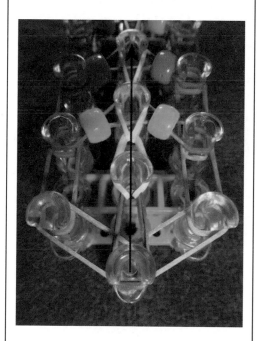

# Step 10

Unhook the left side of the loom. Start at the middle peg and go diagonal to the left, then continue unhooking straight up the loom.

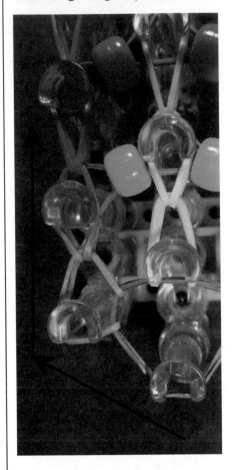

Once you get to the last peg, go diagonal back to the center.

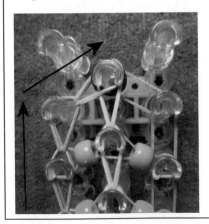

# Step 11

Unhook the right side of the loom. Start at the middle peg and go diagonal to the right, then continue unhooking straight up the loom.

Once you get to the last peg, go diagonal back to the center.

# Step 12

Place an extension band on the end of the bracelet (see common steps for instructions on how to do this.) Leave the loom tool attached to the bracelet.

Remove the bracelet from the loom.

# Step 13

Position the loom with the arrows facing away from you. Place 5 bands going up in a row. It does not matter which row of the loom you decide to use.

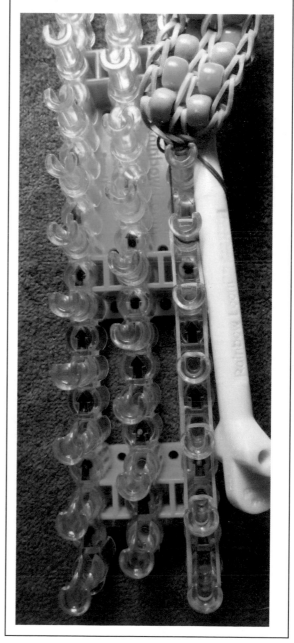

# Step 14

Place the bracelet on the last two pegs of the row using the extension band. Once the bracelet is on the loom, remove the loom tool. Turn the loom so that the arrows are facing towards you.

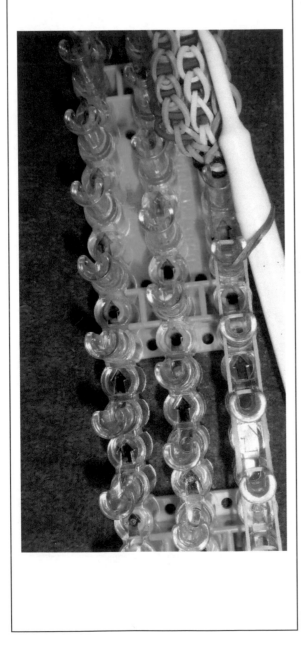

# Step 15

Unhook the extension bracelet. Fasten each end of the bracelet with a c-clip.

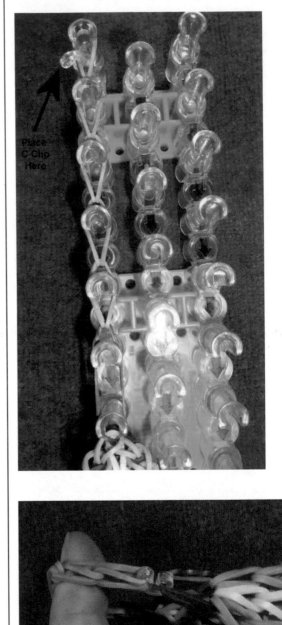

Place C Clip Here

# FLOWER RING

# Step 1

Position the loom so the arrows are facing away from you. Starting at the middle peg place 2 rubber bands going straight up.

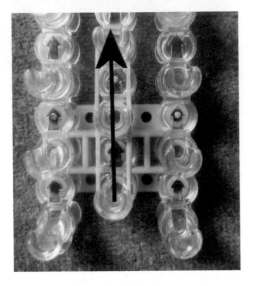

# Step 2

Place one rubber band diaganol to the left. The next band goes straight up and the third band will go diaganol right back to the center.

# Step 3

Repeat step 2 on the right side. Place one rubber band diagonal to the right. The next band will go straight up and the third will go diagonal left back to the center.

# Step 4

Starting at the top center of the hexagon shape we just created, place 2 rubber bands going straight up.

# Step 5

Place the inside hexagon bands, this will be the flower. Bands go from the center out. When placing the bands go in a clockwise direction. Follow the diagram below for the correct placement order.

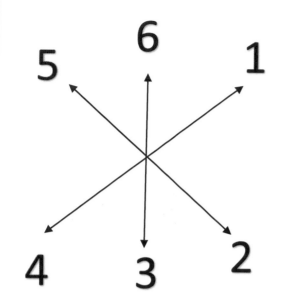

# Step 6

Place an infinity band on the top, bottom and center of the flower.

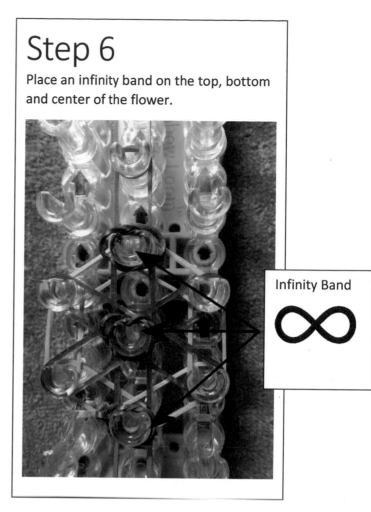

Infinity Band

∞

# Step 7

Turn the loom so that the arrows are now facing you. Begin the unhooking process. Start at the center peg, second from the bottom and go straight up.

# Step 8

Next, we are going to unhook the flower. Start at the bottom of the flower (6 o'clock position) and go straight up.

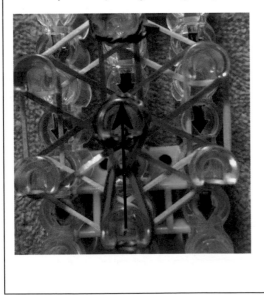

# Step 9

Continue unhooking the flower in a counter clockwise motion. Unhook from the center out. Make sure you gather the band from the inside of the infinity band.

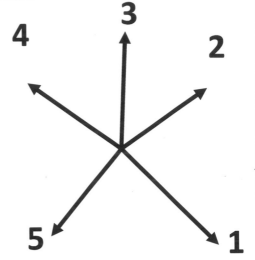

# Step 10

Once the flower is finished. Return to the bottom flower peg (6 o'clock position) to unhook the hexagon shape. Start from the center and unhook diagonal to the left, the next band will go straight up and the third will go diagonal right, back to the center.

# Step 11

Return to the bottom flower peg (6 o'clock position). Continue to unhook the hexagon shape. Start from the center and unhook diagonal to the right, the next band will go straight up and the third will go diagonal left, back to the center.

# Step 12

Go to the top flower peg (12 o'clock position). Unhook the two bands going straight up.

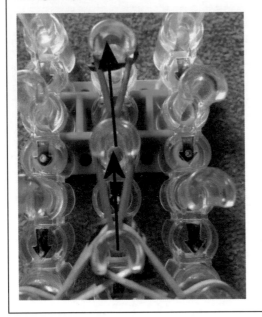

# Step 14

Remove the ring from the loom. And place a C-clip on both ends of the ring.

# Step 13

Place an extension band on the last peg. Make sure the extension band goes around every rubber band on the peg. Leave the loom tool hooked on the extension band.

# FLOWER BRACELET

# Step 1

Position the loom so that the arrows are away from you. Place the rubber bands. Start at the middle peg and go diagonal to the left, then continue straight up the loom.

Once you get to the last peg, go diagonal back to the center.

# Step 2

Place the rubber bands. Start at the middle peg and go diagonal to the right, then continue straight up the loom.

Once you get to the last peg, go diagonal back to the center.

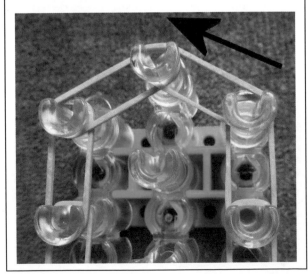

# :ep 3

n the flower pattern. Start at the second
in the center and go in a clockwise
tion until the flower is complete. Always
t in the center and go out.

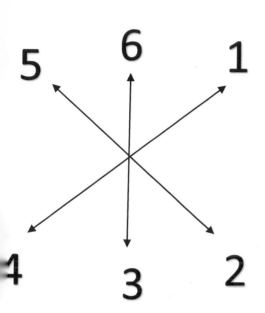

# Step 4

Repeat Step 3 6 times making a flower pattern
up the loom. Start the flower in each position
as outlined in step 3. Always start in the
center and continue in a clockwise motion.

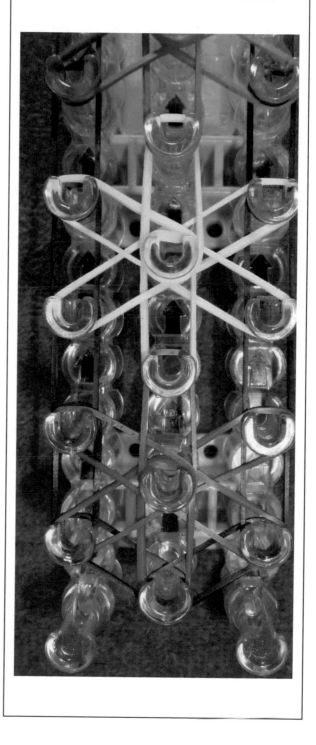

# Step 5

Place an infinity band at each end of the loom as well as the center of each flower.

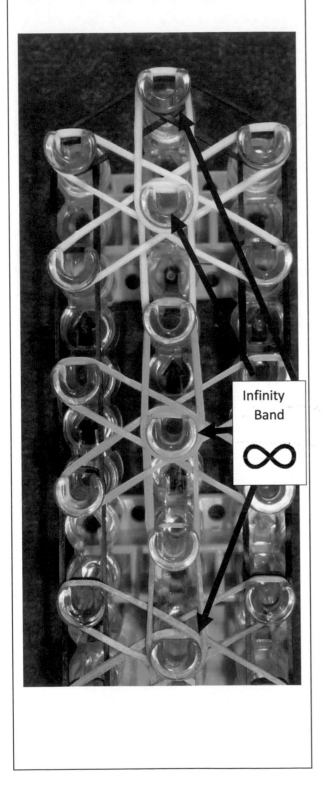

Infinity Band

∞

# Step 6

Turn the loom so that the arrows are now facing towards you. Begin the unhooking process. Start at the first peg in the middle and hook straight up. Make sure you go between the peg and the infinity band. You may need to hold the infinity band down so it does not become unhooked.

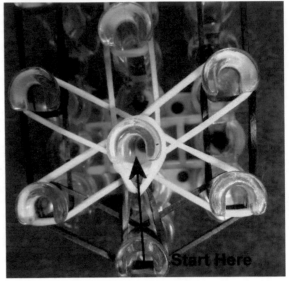

Start Here

Continue unhooking the flower by moving in a counter clockwise motion. Always go from the middle out and go from the inside of the band. See the picture below for the unhooking order.

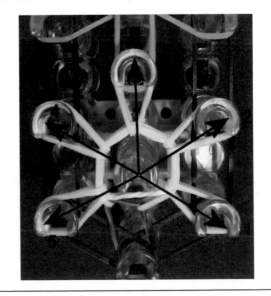

# Step 7

Start the next flower by starting at the bottom of the flower and going straight up.

Continue unhooking the rubber bands in a counter clockwise pattern.

Repeat this step for the remaining 5 flowers. See step 6 for the order to unhook the flower. The order will be the same for each flower. There will be a total of 6 flowers when complete.

# Step 8

Unhook the left side of the loom. Start at the middle peg and go diagonal to the left, then continue unhooking straight up the loom.

Once you get to the last peg, go diagonal back to the center.

# Step 9

Unhook the right side of the loom. Start at the middle peg and go diagonal to the right, then continue unhooking straight up the loom.

Once you get to the last peg, go diagonal back to the center.

# Step 10

Place an extension band on the end of the bracelet (see common steps for instructions on how to do this.)

Remove the bracelet from the loom.

# Step 11

Position the loom with the arrows facing away from you. Place 5 Bands going up in a row. It does not matter which row of the loom you decide to use. Place the bracelet on the last two pegs of the row using the extension band.

# Step 12

Turn the loom so that the arrows are facing towards you. Unhook the bands by going straight up. Place a C-Clip on the last band.

Remove the bracelet from the loom and connect the two ends with a c-clip.

# BEADED FLOWER BRACELET

# Step 1

Position the loom so that the arrows are away from you. Place the rubber bands. Start at the middle peg and go diagonal to the left, then continue straight up the loom.

Once you get to the last peg, go diagonal back to the center.

# Step 2

Place the rubber bands. Start at the middle peg and go diagonal to the right, then continue straight up the loom.

Once you get to the last peg, go diagonal back to the center.

# Step 3

Begin the flower pattern. Start at the second peg in the center and go in a clock wise position until the flower is complete. Always start in the center and go out. See the diagram below for the band placement order.

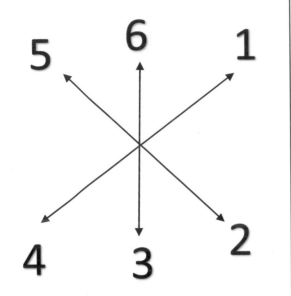

# Step 4

Repeat Step 3 6 times making a flower pattern up the loom. Start the flower in each position as outlined in step 3. Always start in the center and continue in a clockwise motion.

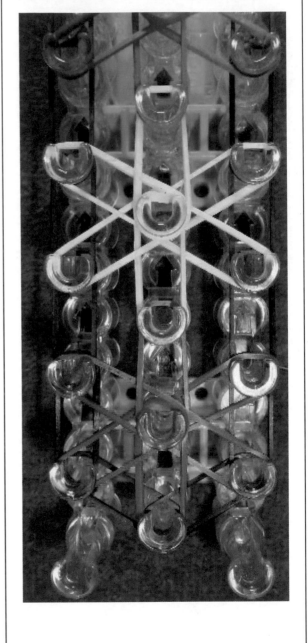

# Step 5

Place an infinity band at each end of the loom as well as the center of each flower.

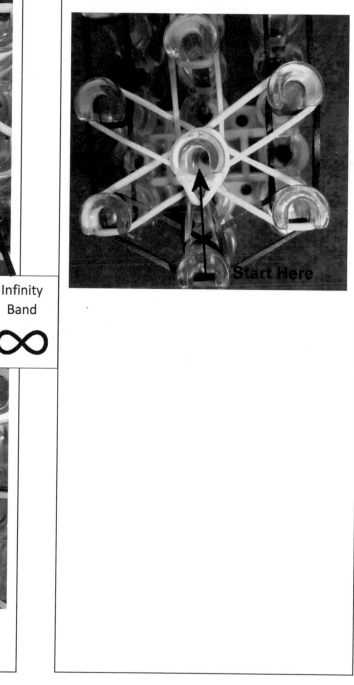

Infinity
Band

∞

# Step 6

Turn the loom so that the arrows are now facing towards you to begin the unhooking process. Start at the first peg in the middle and hook straight up. Make sure you go between the peg and the infinity band. You may need to hold the infinity band down so it does not become unhooked.

Start Here

# Step 7

The bead gets placed onto the rubber band after it gets unhooked, but before it gets placed onto the next peg.

Placing the bead onto the rubber band is the most difficult part of this process. To help facilitate this you can buy a bead tool or you can make your own using a paper clip.

Bend a portion of the paper clip so that you have a straight end to work with.

Place the bead on the straight portion of the paper clip.

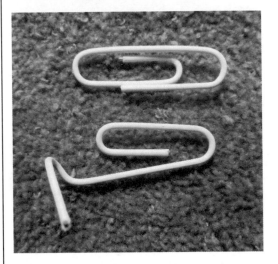

# Step 7a

Using the loom tool unhook the rubber band from the peg. Place the rubber band on the paper clip with the bead. Carefully tilt the paper clip so that the bead slides onto the rubber band.

Place the rubber band onto the next peg.

# Step 7b

Finish unhooking and beading the flowers going in a counter clockwise motion. Follow the numbers in the picture below for the correct unhooking order.

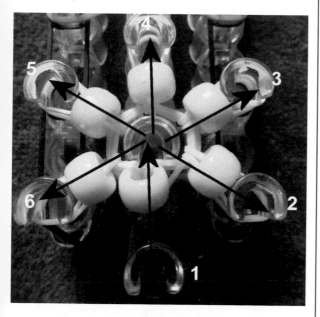

Start the next flower by starting at the bottom of the flower and going straight up.

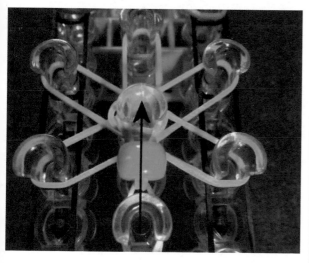

Continue unhooking the rubber bands in a counter clockwise pattern.

# Step 8

Repeat this step for the remaining 5 flowers. There will be a total of 6 flowers when complete.

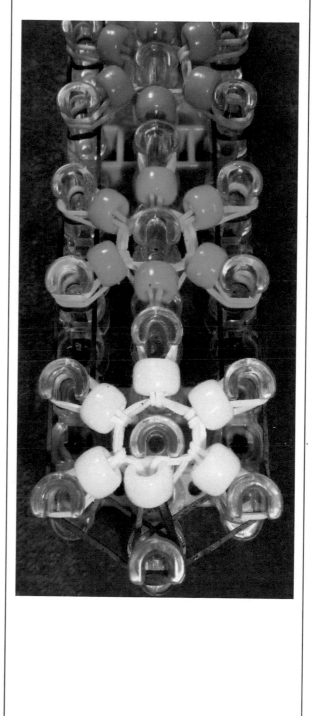

# Step 9

Unhook the left side of the loom. Start at the middle peg and go diagonal to the left, then continue unhooking straight up the loom.

Once you get to the last peg, go diagonal back to the center.

# Step 10

Unhook the left side of the loom. Start at the middle peg and go diagonal to the left, then continue unhooking straight up the loom.

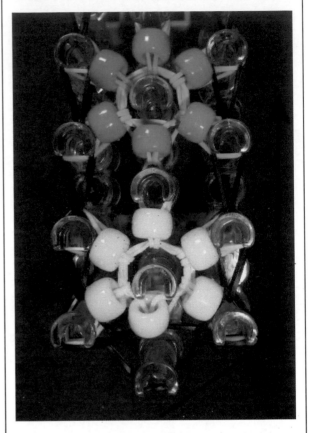

Once you get to the last peg, go diagonal back to the center.

# Step 11

Place an extension band on the end of the loom. Make sure the extension band goes around every rubber band on the last peg. Leave the loom tool hooked onto the band until the extension portion is attached.

Remove the bracelet from the loom.

# Step 12

Position the loom with the arrows facing away from you. Place 5 Bands going up in a row. It does not matter which row of the loom you decide to use.

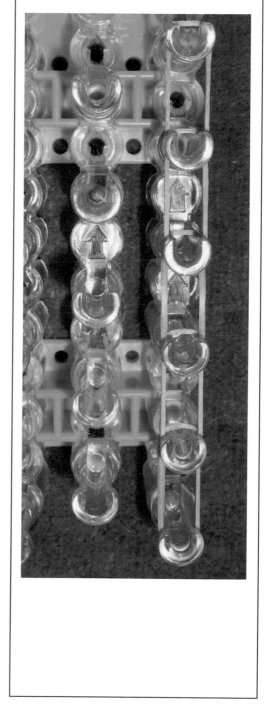

# Step 13

Place the bracelet on the last two pegs of the row using the extension band.

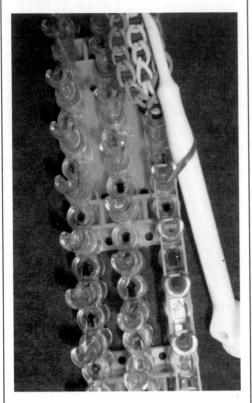

And then turn the loom so that the arrows are facing towards you.

# Step 14

Unhook the extension bracelet. Place a C-Clip on the last band.

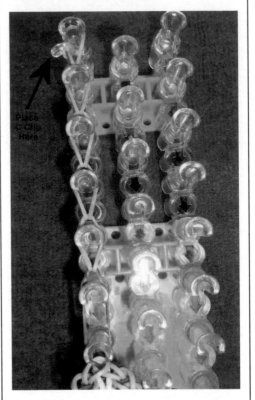

Fasten both ends of the bracelet with the C-Clip.

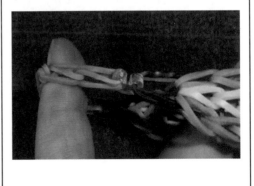

5458835R00026

Made in the USA
San Bernardino, CA
06 November 2013